Editor
Gisela Lee

Managing Editor
Karen Goldfluss, M.S. Ed.

Editor-in-Chief
Sharon Coan, M.S. Ed.

Cover Artist
Barb Lorseyedi

Art Coordinator
Kevin Barnes

Art Director
CJae Froshay

Imaging
Alfred Lau
James Edward Grace

Product Manager
Phil Garcia

Publisher
Mary D. Smith, M.S. Ed.

Money

GRADES 1 & 2

Authors

Teacher Created Resources Staff

Teacher Created Resources, Inc.
6421 Industry Way
Westminster, CA 92683
www.teachercreated.com
ISBN-13: 978-0-7439-3318-6
ISBN-10: 0-7439-3318-4
©2002 Teacher Created Resources, Inc.
Reprinted, 2006
Made in U.S.A.

Table of Contents

Introduction 3
Practice 1: Identifying Money 4
Practice 2: Identifying Money 5
Practice 3: Identifying Money 6
Practice 4: Counting Money and Basic Money Word Problems 7
Practice 5: Counting Money and Basic Money Word Problems 8
Practice 6: Counting Money and Basic Money Word Problems 9
Practice 7: Counting Sets of Coins (Pennies) 10
Practice 8: Counting Coins 11
Practice 9: Counting Coins 12
Practice 10: Counting Sets of Coins (Nickels and Dimes) 13
Practice 11: Counting Money up to a Dollar 14
Practice 12: Counting Money up to a Dollar 15
Practice 13: Counting Money (Pennies, Nickels, Dimes, and Quarters) 16
Practice 14: Adding Money 17
Practice 15: Adding Money 18
Practice 16: Subtracting Money 19
Practice 17: Subtracting Money 20
Practice 18: Comparing Groups of Money 21
Practice 19: Estimating Money 22
Practice 20: Estimating Money 23
Practice 21: Counting Dollars and Cents 24
Practice 22: Using the Dollar Sign 25
Practice 23: Using the Cent and Dollar Sign 26
Practice 24: Money Combination Word Problems 27
Practice 25: Comparing Money Using Greater Than, Less Than, or Equal Signs 28
Practice 26: Comparing Money Using Greater Than, Less Than, or Equal Signs 29
Practice 27: Comparing Money Using Greater Than, Less Than, or Equal Signs 30
Practice 28: Comparing Money Using Greater Than, Less Than, or Equal Signs 31
Practice 29: Comparing Money Using Greater Than, Less Than, or Equal Signs 32
Practice 30: Calculating Money Using Information in Charts 33
Practice 31: Calculating Money Using Information in Charts 34
Practice 32: Calculating Money Using Information in Tables 35
Practice 33: Calculating Money Using Information in Tables 36
Practice 34: Basic Money Word Problems 37
Practice 35: Calculating Prices 38
Practice 36: Complex Money Word Problems 39
Test Practice 1 40
Test Practice 2 41
Test Practice 3 42
Test Practice 4 43
Test Practice 5 44
Test Practice 6 45
Answer Sheet 46
Answer Key 47

Introduction

The old adage "practice makes perfect" can really hold true for your child and his or her education. The more practice and exposure your child has with concepts being taught in school, the more success he or she is likely to find. For many parents, knowing how to help their children can be frustrating because the resources may not be readily available. As a parent it is also difficult to know where to focus your efforts so that the extra practice your child receives at home supports what he or she is learning in school.

This book has been designed to help parents and teachers reinforce basic skills with their children. *Practice Makes Perfect* reviews basic math skills for children in the first and second grades. The math focus is on money. While it would be impossible to include all concepts taught in the first and second grades in this book, the following basic objectives are reinforced through practice exercises. These objectives support math standards established on a district, state, or national level. (Refer to the Table of Contents for the specific objectives of each practice page.)

- identifying and counting different types of money
- word problems
- adding and subtracting money
- understanding graphs, charts, and tables with relation to money
- inequality signs with relation to money

There are 36 practice pages organized sequentially, so children can build their knowledge from more basic skills to higher-level math skills. To correct the practice pages in this book, use the answer key provided on pages 47 and 48. Six practice tests follow the practice pages. These provide children with multiple-choice test items to help prepare them for standardized tests administered in schools. As children complete a problem, they fill in the correct letter among the answer choices. An optional "bubble-in" answer sheet has also been provided on page 46. This answer sheet is similar to those found on standardized tests. As your child completes each test, he or she can fill in the correct bubbles on the answer sheet.

How to Make the Most of This Book

Here are some useful ideas for optimizing the practice pages in this book:

- Set aside a specific place in your home to work on the practice pages. Keep it neat and tidy with materials on hand.

- Set up a certain time of day to work on the practice pages. This will establish consistency. An alternative is to look for times in your day or week that are less hectic and conducive to practicing skills.

- Keep all practice sessions with your child positive and constructive. If the mood becomes tense or you and your child are frustrated, set the book aside and look for another time to practice with your child.

- Help with instructions if necessary. If your child is having difficulty understanding what to do or how to get started, work through the first problem with him or her.

- Review the work your child has done. This serves as reinforcement and provides further practice.

- Allow your child to use whatever writing instruments he or she prefers. For example, colored pencils can add variety and pleasure to drill work.

- Pay attention to the areas in which your child has the most difficulty. Provide extra guidance and exercises in those areas. Allowing children to use drawings and manipulatives, such as coins, tiles, game markers, or flash cards can help them grasp difficult concepts more easily.

- Look for ways to make real-life application to the skills being reinforced.

Practice 1

1. Which one is a quarter?

   (A)   (B)    (C)   (D)

2. Which one is a penny?

   (A)   (B)   (C)    (D)

3. Which one is a nickel?

   (A)   (B)   (C)   (D)

4. Which one is a dime?

   (A)   (B)   (C)   (D)

5. Name the coin.

   _____

6. Name the coin.

   _____

Practice 2

1. How many are quarters?

_____

2. How many are pennies?

_____

3. How many are dimes?

_____

Practice 3

1. How many cents?

_____

2. How many cents?

_____

3. How many cents?

_____

4. How many cents?

_____

5. Name the two coins.

_____

_____

6. Name the two coins.

_____

_____

7. Name the three coins.

_____

_____

_____

Practice 4

1. Write the number of cents. _____ ¢	2. Write the number of cents. _____ ¢	3. Write the number of cents. _____ ¢

4. Xavier found 6¢ in his shirt pocket and 3¢ in his jacket pocket. How much money did Xavier find in all? Xavier found _____ ¢ in all.	5. Maria had 5¢ in her piggy bank and 3¢ in her purse. How much money did Maria have in all? Maria had _____ ¢ in all.

6. Write the number of cents.  _____ ¢	7. Write the number of cents. _____ ¢	8. Write the number of cents. _____ ¢

9. I have 2 coins that make exactly 6¢. One of the coins is a nickel. What is the other coin? _____	10. I have 2 coins that make exactly 10¢. Both of the coins are the same. What are the 2 coins that I have? _____

Practice 5

1. Write the number of cents.

_____ ¢

2. Write the number of cents.

_____ ¢

3. Write the number of cents.

_____ ¢

4. Ashley has a quarter and a nickel in her pocket. How much money does she have in all?

Ashley has_____ ¢ in all.

5. Vincent had 35¢. He spent 10¢ buying a marble. How much money does Vincent have left?

Vincent has _____ ¢ left.

6. Write the number of cents.

_____ ¢

7. Write the number of cents.

_____ ¢

8. Write the number of cents.

_____ ¢

9. Imani had a dime and 2 nickels. How much money did she have in all?

Imani had _____ ¢ in all.

10. Esperanza had 2 quarters and 1 penny. How much money did she have in all?

Esperanza had _____ ¢ in all.

Practice 6

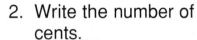

1. Write the number of cents.   _____ ¢	2. Write the number of cents.  _____ ¢	3. Write the number of cents.  _____ ¢

4. Imogene has 3 dimes. How much money does she have? Does she have enough to buy a 25¢ pencil?

   Imogene has _____ ¢.

   Yes   No

5. Franklin has a quarter, a dime, and a penny. How much money does he have in all? Does he have enough to buy a 50¢ cookie?

   Franklin has _____ ¢.

   Yes   No

6. Write the number of cents.  _____ ¢	7. Write the number of cents.  _____ ¢	8. Write the number of cents. 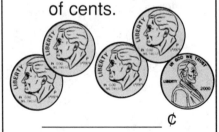 _____ ¢

9. I have one quarter. How many nickels does it take to make one quarter?

   It takes _____ nickels to make one quarter.

10. I have one quarter. How many pennies does it take to make one quarter?

   It takes _____ pennies to make one quarter.

Practice 7

1. Which set shows 5¢?

(A)

(B)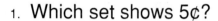

(C)

3. Which set shows 8¢?

(A)

(B)

(C)

2. Which set shows 4¢?

(A)

(B)

(C)

4. Which set shows 7¢?

(A)

(B)

(C)

Practice 8

1. How much money do you have?

    (A) 30¢   (B) 45¢   (C) 15¢   (D) 25¢

2. How much money do you have?

    (A) 45¢   (B) 40¢   (C) 55¢   (D) 50¢

3. How much money do you have?

    (A) 35¢   (B) 10¢   (C) 25¢   (D) 15¢

4. How much money do you have?

    (A) 40¢   (B) 35¢   (C) 45¢   (D) 50¢

5. How much money do you have?

    (A) 25¢   (B) 30¢   (C) 40¢   (D) 35¢

Practice 9

1. How much money do you have?

   (A) 20¢   (B) 5¢   (C) 15¢   (D) 25¢

2. How much money do you have?

   (A) 50¢   (B) 35¢   (C) 45¢   (D) 40¢

3. How much money do you have?

   (A) 60¢   (B) 55¢   (C) 50¢   (D) 65¢

4. How much money do you have?

   (A) 75¢   (B) 50¢   (C) 45¢   (D) 40¢

5. How much money do you have?

   (A) 40¢   (B) 45¢   (C) 35¢   (D) 50¢

Practice 10

1. Which set shows 50¢?

   (A)

   (B)

   (C)

2. Which set shows 25¢?

   (A)

   (B)

   (C)

3. Which set shows 70¢?

   (A)

   (B)

   (C)

Practice 11

1. How much money do you have? _____

2. How much money do you have? _____

3. How much money do you have? _____

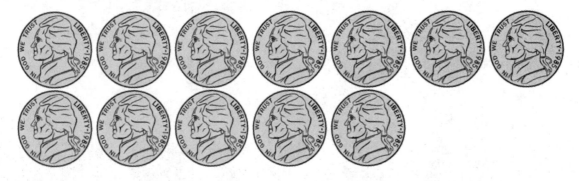

4. How much money do you have? _____

5. How much money do you have? _____

Practice 12

1. How much money is this? _____

2. How much money is this? _____

3. How much money is this? _____

4. How much money is this? _____

Practice 13

1. How much money do you have? _____¢

2. How much money do you have? _____¢

3. How much money do you have? _____¢

4. How much money do you have? _____¢

Practice 14

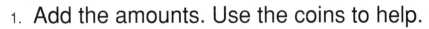

1. Add the amounts. Use the coins to help.

45¢ + 1¢ = _____¢

(A) 46¢   (B) 48¢   (C) 43¢   (D) 44¢

2. Add the amounts. Use the coins to help.

31¢ + 22¢ = _____¢

(A) 28¢   (B) 33¢   (C) 29¢   (D) 53¢

3. Add the amounts. Use the coins to help.

21¢ + 6¢ = _____¢

(A) 27¢   (B) 26¢   (C) 14¢   (D) 15¢

4. Add the amounts. Use the coins to help.

21¢ + 7¢ = _____¢

(A) 14¢   (B) 27¢   (C) 28¢   (D) 13¢

Practice 15

1. Add the amounts. Use the coins to help.

41¢ + 2¢ = _____¢

(A) 37¢   (B) 38¢   (C) 43¢   (D) 46¢

---

2. Add the amounts. Use the coins to help.

27¢ + 11¢ = _____¢

(A) 38¢   (B) 15¢   (C) 38¢   (D) 16¢

---

3. Add the amounts. Use the coins to help.

11¢ + 15¢ = _____¢

(A) 17¢   (B) 7¢   (C) 6¢   (D) 26¢

---

4. Add the amounts. Use the coins to help.

22¢ + 25¢ = _____¢

(A) 47¢   (B) 46¢   (C) 4¢   (D) 3¢

Practice 16

1. Subtract the amounts. Use the coins to help.

35¢ – 3¢ = _____ ¢

2. Subtract the amounts. Use the coins to help.

22¢ – 2¢ = _____ ¢

3. Subtract the amounts. Use the coins to help.

30¢ – 2¢ = _____ ¢

4. Subtract the amounts. Use the coins to help.

21¢ – 3¢ = _____ ¢

Practice 17

1. Subtract the amounts. Use the coins to help.

31¢ – 21¢ = _____ ¢

---

2. Subtract the amounts. Use the coins to help.

12¢ – 3¢ = _____ ¢

---

3. Subtract the amounts. Use the coins to help.

26¢ – 6¢ = _____ ¢

---

4. Subtract the amounts. Use the coins to help.

14¢ – 11¢ = _____ ¢

Practice 18

1. Which group shows *more than* 39¢?

   (A)    (B)

2. Which group shows *more than* 54¢?

   (A)    (B)

3. Which group shows *more than* 44¢?

   (A)   (B)

4. Which group shows *more than* 49¢?

   (A)   (B)

5. Which group shows *more than* 65¢?

   (A)

   (B)

Practice 19

1. Estimate the amount.

   (A) *more than* 60¢   (B) *less than* 35¢   (C) *about* 50¢

2. Estimate the amount.

   (A) *more than* 60¢   (B) *less than* 35¢   (C) *about* 50¢

3. Estimate the amount.

   (A) *less than* 10¢   (B) *about* 10¢   (C) *more than* 20¢

4. Estimate the amount.

   (A) *more than* 50¢   (B) *less than* 30¢   (C) *about* 40¢

Practice 20

1. Estimate. Is this worth *less than* 50¢?

Write *yes* or *no.* _____

2. Estimate. Is this worth *less than* 80¢?

Write *yes* or *no.* _____

3. Estimate. Is this worth *more than* 40¢?

Write *yes* or *no.* _____

4. Estimate. Is this worth *less than* 95¢?

Write *yes* or *no.* _____

Practice 2

Write the letter o _____ swer on the line.

_____ 1. (10¢)   **A.** $1.25

_____ 2. | $1 | (25¢) (10¢) (10¢)   **B.**   35¢

_____ 3. (25¢) (25¢) (10¢) (1¢) (1¢)   **C.**   85¢

_____ 4. (25¢) (10¢)   **D.**   47¢

_____ 5. (25¢) (25¢) (5¢)   **E.**   15¢

_____ 6. (25¢) (1¢) (1¢)   **F.**   62¢

_____ 7. (25¢) (25¢) (25¢) (10¢)   **G.**   27¢

_____ 8. | $1 | (25¢)   **H.**   9¢

_____ 9. (25¢) (10¢) (10¢) (1¢) (1¢)   **I.** $1.45

_____ 10. (5¢) (1¢) (1¢) (1¢) (1¢)   **J.**   55¢

Practice 22

1. Write 52¢ using a dollar sign.
   (A) $52.00   (B) $0.52   (C) $1.52   (D) $5.20

2. Write 70¢ using a dollar sign.
   (A) $1.70   (B) $7.00   (C) $70.00   (D) $0.70

3. Write 116¢ using a dollar sign.
   (A) $2.16   (B) $11.60   (C) $1.16   (D) $116.00

4. Write the amount using a dollar sign. _____

5. Write the amount using a dollar sign. _____

6. Write the amount using a dollar sign. _____

Practice 23

1. Write the amount using a cent sign. _____

2. Write the amount using a cent sign. _____

3. Write the amount using a dollar sign. _____

4. Write the amount using a dollar sign. _____

Practice 24 ❧ ❧ ❧ ❧ ❧ ❧ ❧ ❧ ❧ ❧ ❧ ❧ ❧

1. You have one dollar, five quarters, seven dimes, one nickel, and five pennies. How much money do you have?

    (A) $4.05   (B) $3.00   (C) $3.05   (D) $3.30

2. You have two dollars, seven quarters, three nickels, and seven pennies. How much money do you have?

    (A) $4.97   (B) $3.92   (C) $4.22   (D) $3.97

3. You have three dollars, six quarters, one dime, two nickels, and one penny. How much money do you have?

    (A) $4.66   (B) $5.71   (C) $4.71   (D) $4.46

4. You have one dollar, four quarters, one dime, five nickels, and nine pennies. How much money do you have?

    (A) $2.49   (B) $3.44   (C) $2.44   (D) $2.19

5. You have one dollar, six quarters, three nickels, and two pennies. How much money do you have?

    (A) $2.92   (B) $2.62   (C) $1.67   (D) $2.67

6. You have two dollars, five quarters, seven dimes, four nickels, and five pennies. How much money do you have?

    (A) $4.20   (B) $4.25   (C) $3.20   (D) $4.45

7. You have two dollars, two quarters, five dimes, and four pennies. How much money do you have?

    (A) $3.09   (B) $3.04   (C) $4.04   (D) $2.79

Practice 25

1. Compare the price of each item. Which answer is correct?

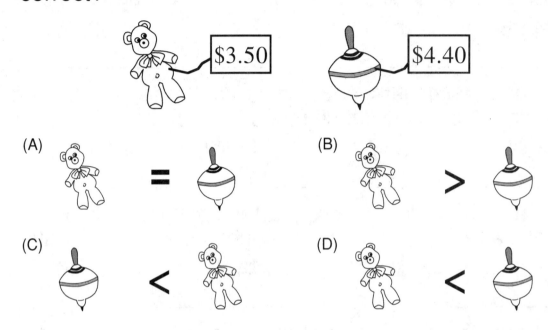

2. Compare the price of each item. Which answer is correct?

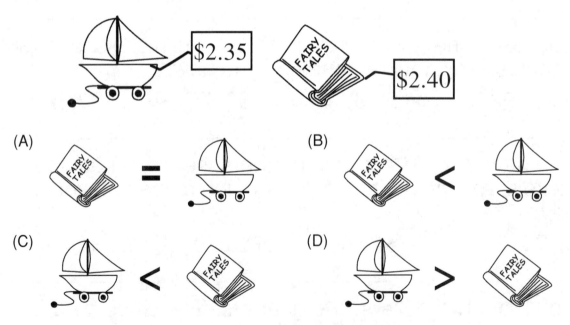

Practice 26

1. Compare the price for each item. Which answer is correct?

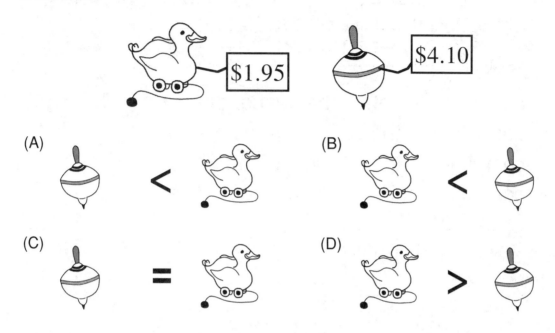

2. Compare the price of each item. Which answer is correct?

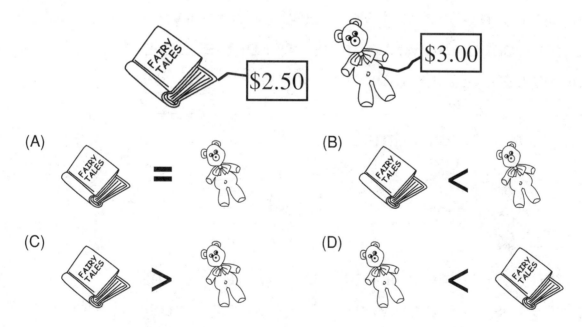

Practice 27

1. Which statement is true?

$1.31 $1.44

  (A) the cost of the paints < the cost of the car

  (B) the cost of car = the cost of the paints

  (C) the cost of the car > the cost of the paints

  (D) the cost of the paints > the cost of the car

2. Which statement is true?

$1.17 $1.23

  (A) the cost of the yo-yo > the cost of the trumpet

  (B) the cost of trumpet = the cost of the yo-yo

  (C) the cost of the yo-yo < the cost of the trumpet

  (D) the cost of the trumpet > the cost of the yo-yo

3. Which statement is true?

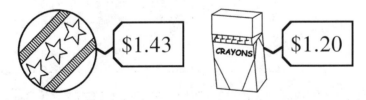

$1.43 $1.20

  (A) the cost of the ball < the cost of the crayons

  (B) the cost of the crayons > the cost of the ball

  (C) the cost of ball = the cost of the crayons

  (D) the cost of the ball > the cost of the crayons

Practice 28

1. Write < or > in the circle to compare the amounts.

2. Write < or > in the circle to compare the amounts.

3. Write < or > in the circle to compare the amounts.

4. Write < or > in the circle to compare the amounts.

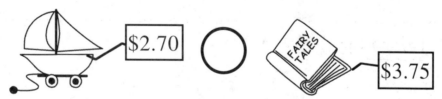

5. Write < or > in the circle to compare the amounts.

Practice 29

1. Write < or > in the circle to compare the amounts.

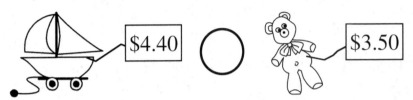

2. Write < or > in the circle to compare the amounts.

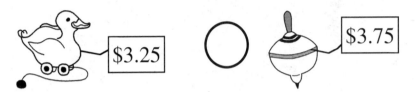

3. Write < or > in the circle to compare the amounts.

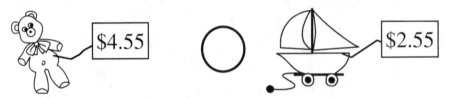

4. Write < or > in the circle to compare the amounts.

5. Write < or > in the circle to compare the amounts.

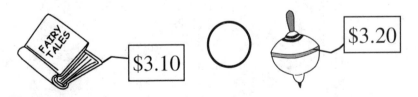

Practice 30

1. The chart shows the total number of coins. What amount is shown on the chart?

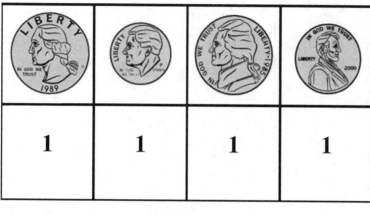

(A) 41¢   (B) 31¢   (C) 40¢   (D) 36¢

2. The chart shows the total number of coins. What amount is shown on the chart?

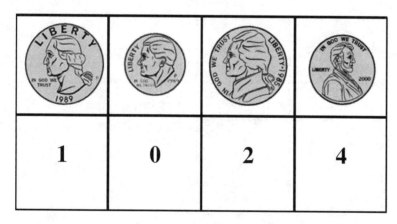

(A) 38¢   (B) 39¢   (C) 49¢   (D) 44¢

Practice 31

1. The chart shows the total number of coins. What amount is shown on the chart?

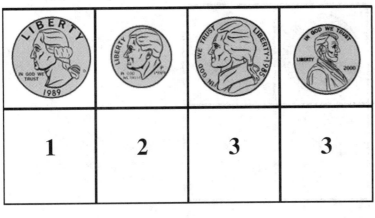

(A) 64¢   (B) 63¢   (C) 68¢   (D) 73¢

---

2. The chart shows the total number of coins. What amount is shown on the chart?

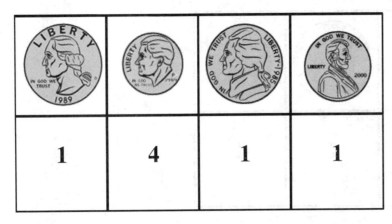

(A) 81¢   (B) 66¢   (C) 72¢   (D) 71¢

Practice 32

1. The chart shows the total number of coins. What amount is shown on the chart?

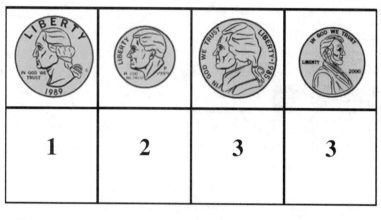

1	2	3	3

(A) 64¢   (B) 63¢   (C) 68¢   (D) 73¢

---

2. The chart shows the total number of coins. What amount is shown on the chart?

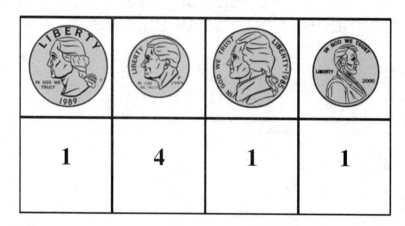

1	4	1	1

(A) 81¢   (B) 66¢   (C) 72¢   (D) 71¢

Practice 33

1. The table shows how many of each coin Mike has in his bank. How much money does Mike have?

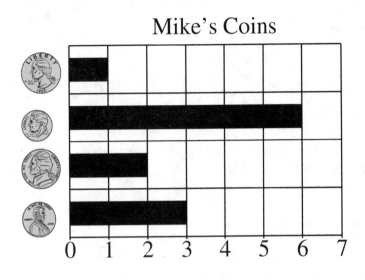

Mike's Coins

(A) 8¢   (B) 73¢   (C) 98¢   (D) 99¢

2. The table shows how many of each coin Stephanie has in her bank. How much money does Stephanie have?

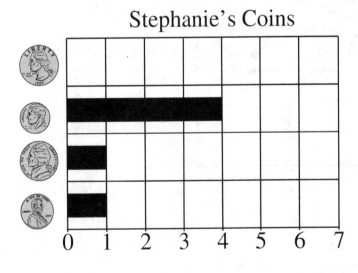

Stephanie's Coins

(A) 36¢   (B) 71¢   (C) 46¢   (D) 47¢

Practice 34

1. Floyd has 4 dimes. Can he buy a pencil that costs 25¢?

    yes   no

2. Tracy has 5 dimes. Can she buy a notebook that costs $1.25?

    yes   no

3. Jose has 6 nickels. How much money does he have?

    Jose has _____ ¢.

4. Rosa has 3 nickels. How much money does she have?

    Rosa has _____ ¢.

5. Artie has 4 dimes and 2 pennies. How much money does Artie have in all?

    Artie has _____ ¢ in all.

6. Glenda has 5 nickels and 1 penny. How much money does Glenda have in all?

    Glenda has _____ ¢ in all.

7. Aimee had $1.40. She spent $1.10 at the grocery store. How much money does Aimee have left?

    Aimee has $ _____ left.

8. Bailey had $1.95. He spent $0.85 at the movies. How much money does Bailey have left?

    Bailey has $ _____ left.

Practice 35

Directions: Each item costs a different amount of money. What is the price of each item? Count the money and write the price on the line. Remember to use the decimal point in each answer.

1. 1 dollar 2 quarters 1 nickel 1 penny A bag of popcorn costs $ _____	**5.** 2 dollars 2 quarters 3 dimes A box of crayons costs $ _____
2. 5 dollars 2 dimes 1 nickel A yo-yo costs $ _____	**6.** 2 dollars 3 quarters 3 nickels 9 pennies A small teddy bear costs $ _____
3. 3 dollars 2 dimes 3 nickels A puzzles and games book costs $ _____	**7.** 5 dollars 3 quarters A flower pot costs $ _____
4. 4 dollars 1 quarter 5 pennies A jump rope costs $ _____	**8.** 2 dollars 3 dimes 1 nickel A deck of cards costs $ _____

Practice 36

Directions: Read each word problem. Solve each problem by calculating the amount of change each person will receive. Circle the correct answer. On a separate sheet of paper, check each answer by adding the calculated change and the price of the item purchased. The total should be the same amount of money that each person had to spend.

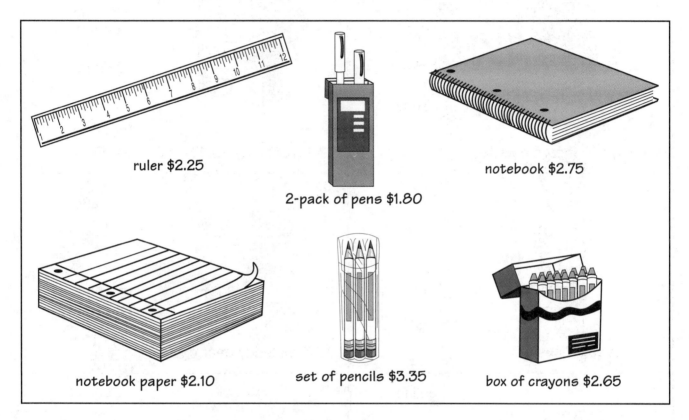

ruler $2.25

2-pack of pens $1.80

notebook $2.75

notebook paper $2.10

set of pencils $3.35

box of crayons $2.65

1. Jason has $3.65. He buys a 2-pack of pens. How much change is Jason given?   **$1.85**   **$2.00**

2. Pam has $2.50. She buys notebook paper. How much change is Pam given?   **$0.40**   **$1.40**

3. Christie has $4.95. She buys a notebook and 2-pack of pens. How much change is Christie given?   **$0.40**   **$1.20**

4. John has $4.75. He buys a set of pencils. How much change is John given?   **$5.00**   **$1.40**

5. Mara has $6.85. She buys a ruler and a notebook. How much change is Mara given?   **$1.85**   **$2.85**

Test Practice 1 ♪ ♪ ♪ ♪ ♪ ♪ ♪ ♪ ♪ ♪ ♪

Solve each problem and fill in the correct circle that matches each answer.

1.

(A) 10¢
(B) 5¢
(C) 1¢
(D) 25¢

6.

(A) 10¢
(B) 20¢
(C) 15¢
(D) 25¢

2.

(A) 1¢
(B) 25¢
(C) 10¢
(D) 5¢

7.

(A) 23¢
(B) 24¢
(C) 25¢
(D) 26¢

3.

(A) 5¢
(B) 10¢
(C) 25¢
(D) 1¢

8.

(A) 8¢
(B) 6¢
(C) 10¢
(D) 4¢

4.

(A) 5¢
(B) 10¢
(C) 1¢
(D) 25¢

9.

(A) 15¢
(B) 10¢
(C) 20¢
(D) 25¢

5.

(A) 10¢
(B) 11¢
(C) 12¢
(D) 13¢

10.

(A) 50¢
(B) 60¢
(C) 40¢
(D) 30¢

Test Practice 2

Solve each problem and fill in the correct circle that matches each answer.

1.
   Ⓐ 10¢
   Ⓑ 20¢
   Ⓒ 30¢
   Ⓓ 40¢

2.
   Ⓐ 10¢
   Ⓑ 30¢
   Ⓒ 15¢
   Ⓓ 25¢

3.
   Ⓐ 20¢
   Ⓑ 10¢
   Ⓒ 40¢
   Ⓓ 30¢

4.
   Ⓐ 15¢
   Ⓑ 20¢
   Ⓒ 25¢
   Ⓓ 30¢

5.
   Ⓐ 25¢
   Ⓑ 26¢
   Ⓒ 27¢
   Ⓓ 28¢

6.
   Ⓐ 12¢
   Ⓑ 11¢
   Ⓒ 10¢
   Ⓓ 13¢

7.
   Ⓐ 15¢
   Ⓑ 20¢
   Ⓒ 25¢
   Ⓓ 30¢

8.
   Ⓐ 85¢
   Ⓑ 65¢
   Ⓒ 70¢
   Ⓓ 75¢

9.
   Ⓐ 30¢
   Ⓑ 40¢
   Ⓒ 35¢
   Ⓓ 45¢

10.
    Ⓐ 40¢
    Ⓑ 45¢
    Ⓒ 50¢
    Ⓓ 55¢

Test Practice 3 ම ම ම ම ම ම ම ම ම ම

Solve each problem and fill in the correct circle that matches each answer.

1.

1 dime = _____ nickels

Ⓐ 2
Ⓑ 3
Ⓒ 4
Ⓓ 5

6.

5 nickels = _____ quarter

Ⓐ 2
Ⓑ 4
Ⓒ 1
Ⓓ 5

2.

1 quarter = _____ nickels

Ⓐ 5
Ⓑ 6
Ⓒ 7
Ⓓ 8

7.

3 dimes = _____ nickels

Ⓐ 9
Ⓑ 8
Ⓒ 7
Ⓓ 6

3.

1 nickel = _____ pennies

Ⓐ 1
Ⓑ 3
Ⓒ 5
Ⓓ 7

8.

1 dime = _____ pennies

Ⓐ 10
Ⓑ 20
Ⓒ 30
Ⓓ 40

4.

5 dimes = _____ quarters

Ⓐ 1
Ⓑ 2
Ⓒ 3
Ⓓ 4

9.

1 quarter = _____ pennies

Ⓐ 15
Ⓑ 25
Ⓒ 35
Ⓓ 45

5.

one dollar = _____ quarters

Ⓐ 4
Ⓑ 3
Ⓒ 2
Ⓓ 1

10.

one dollar = _____ dimes

Ⓐ 1
Ⓑ 4
Ⓒ 10
Ⓓ 20

#3318 Practice Makes Perfect: Money

Test Practice 4 ੭ ੭ ੭ ੭ ੭ ੭ ੭ ੭ ੭ ੭ ੭ ੭

Solve each problem and fill in the correct circle that matches each answer.

1. 2¢
    + 10¢

    (A) 8¢
    (B) 10¢
    (C) 12¢
    (D) 14¢

6. 19¢
    + 11¢

    (A) 20¢
    (B) 30¢
    (C) 40¢
    (D) 50¢

2. 15¢
    + 3¢

    (A) 16¢
    (B) 17¢
    (C) 18¢
    (D) 19¢

7. 70¢
    + 5¢

    (A) 65¢
    (B) 55¢
    (C) 75¢
    (D) 85¢

3. 20¢
    + 10¢

    (A) 40¢
    (B) 30¢
    (C) 20¢
    (D) 50¢

8. 24¢
    + 6¢

    (A) 20¢
    (B) 30¢
    (C) 40¢
    (D) 50¢

4. 17¢
    + 13¢

    (A) 20¢
    (B) 30¢
    (C) 40¢
    (D) 50¢

9. 39¢
    + 12¢

    (A) 51¢
    (B) 52¢
    (C) 53¢
    (D) 54¢

5. 40¢
    + 4¢

    (A) 44¢
    (B) 54¢
    (C) 34¢
    (D) 64¢

10. 50¢
    + 12¢

    (A) 52¢
    (B) 72¢
    (C) 42¢
    (D) 62¢

Test Practice 5 ༊ ༄ ༊ ༄ ༊ ༄ ༊ ༄ ༊ ༄ ༊ ༄

Solve each problem and fill in the correct circle that matches each answer.

1.　　17¢
　　 − 11¢

(A) 6¢
(B) 8¢
(C) 5¢
(D) 7¢

6.　　75¢
　　 − 25¢

(A) 50¢
(B) 60¢
(C) 70¢
(D) 80¢

2.　　10¢
　　 − 5¢

(A) 15¢
(B) 12¢
(C) 5¢
(D) 3¢

7.　　48¢
　　 − 12¢

(A) 36¢
(B) 26¢
(C) 16¢
(D) 46¢

3.　　25¢
　　 − 8¢

(A) 16¢
(B) 17¢
(C) 18¢
(D) 19¢

8.　　60¢
　　 − 15¢

(A) 35¢
(B) 55¢
(C) 45¢
(D) 25¢

4.　　11¢
　　 − 2¢

(A) 6¢
(B) 7¢
(C) 8¢
(D) 9¢

9.　　54¢
　　 − 6¢

(A) 38¢
(B) 48¢
(C) 28¢
(D) 58¢

5.　　30¢
　　 − 10¢

(A) 20¢
(B) 40¢
(C) 10¢
(D) 30¢

10.　　45¢
　　 − 10¢

(A) 25¢
(B) 15¢
(C) 35¢
(D) 45¢

 #3318 Practice Makes Perfect: Money

Test Practice 6

Solve each problem and fill in the correct circle that matches each answer.

1. $1.00
   + $3.00
   - Ⓐ $4.00
   - Ⓑ $5.00
   - Ⓒ $6.00
   - Ⓓ $7.00

2. $0.75
   + $0.25
   - Ⓐ $2.00
   - Ⓑ $3.00
   - Ⓒ $1.00
   - Ⓓ $4.00

3. $10.00
   + $12.00
   - Ⓐ $2.00
   - Ⓑ $32.00
   - Ⓒ $12.00
   - Ⓓ $22.00

4. $15.00
   + $5.00
   - Ⓐ $20.00
   - Ⓑ $30.00
   - Ⓒ $10.00
   - Ⓓ $40.00

5. $0.45
   + $0.60
   - Ⓐ $1.00
   - Ⓑ $1.15
   - Ⓒ $1.20
   - Ⓓ $1.05

6. $0.45
   − $0.15
   - Ⓐ $0.30
   - Ⓑ $0.20
   - Ⓒ $0.40
   - Ⓓ $0.60

7. $11.00
   − $3.00
   - Ⓐ $8.00
   - Ⓑ $9.00
   - Ⓒ $10.00
   - Ⓓ $7.00

8. $17.00
   − $14.00
   - Ⓐ $2.00
   - Ⓑ $3.00
   - Ⓒ $4.00
   - Ⓓ $5.00

9. $35.00
   − $17.00
   - Ⓐ $18.00
   - Ⓑ $28.00
   - Ⓒ $38.00
   - Ⓓ $48.00

10. $0.95
    − $0.20
    - Ⓐ $0.65
    - Ⓑ $0.75
    - Ⓒ $0.85
    - Ⓓ $0.55

Answer Sheet

Test Practice 1

1. Ⓐ Ⓑ Ⓒ Ⓓ
2. Ⓐ Ⓑ Ⓒ Ⓓ
3. Ⓐ Ⓑ Ⓒ Ⓓ
4. Ⓐ Ⓑ Ⓒ Ⓓ
5. Ⓐ Ⓑ Ⓒ Ⓓ
6. Ⓐ Ⓑ Ⓒ Ⓓ
7. Ⓐ Ⓑ Ⓒ Ⓓ
8. Ⓐ Ⓑ Ⓒ Ⓓ
9. Ⓐ Ⓑ Ⓒ Ⓓ
10. Ⓐ Ⓑ Ⓒ Ⓓ

Test Practice 2

1. Ⓐ Ⓑ Ⓒ Ⓓ
2. Ⓐ Ⓑ Ⓒ Ⓓ
3. Ⓐ Ⓑ Ⓒ Ⓓ
4. Ⓐ Ⓑ Ⓒ Ⓓ
5. Ⓐ Ⓑ Ⓒ Ⓓ
6. Ⓐ Ⓑ Ⓒ Ⓓ
7. Ⓐ Ⓑ Ⓒ Ⓓ
8. Ⓐ Ⓑ Ⓒ Ⓓ
9. Ⓐ Ⓑ Ⓒ Ⓓ
10. Ⓐ Ⓑ Ⓒ Ⓓ

Test Practice 3

1. Ⓐ Ⓑ Ⓒ Ⓓ
2. Ⓐ Ⓑ Ⓒ Ⓓ
3. Ⓐ Ⓑ Ⓒ Ⓓ
4. Ⓐ Ⓑ Ⓒ Ⓓ
5. Ⓐ Ⓑ Ⓒ Ⓓ
6. Ⓐ Ⓑ Ⓒ Ⓓ
7. Ⓐ Ⓑ Ⓒ Ⓓ
8. Ⓐ Ⓑ Ⓒ Ⓓ
9. Ⓐ Ⓑ Ⓒ Ⓓ
10. Ⓐ Ⓑ Ⓒ Ⓓ

Test Practice 4

1. Ⓐ Ⓑ Ⓒ Ⓓ
2. Ⓐ Ⓑ Ⓒ Ⓓ
3. Ⓐ Ⓑ Ⓒ Ⓓ
4. Ⓐ Ⓑ Ⓒ Ⓓ
5. Ⓐ Ⓑ Ⓒ Ⓓ
6. Ⓐ Ⓑ Ⓒ Ⓓ
7. Ⓐ Ⓑ Ⓒ Ⓓ
8. Ⓐ Ⓑ Ⓒ Ⓓ
9. Ⓐ Ⓑ Ⓒ Ⓓ
10. Ⓐ Ⓑ Ⓒ Ⓓ

Test Practice 5

1. Ⓐ Ⓑ Ⓒ Ⓓ
2. Ⓐ Ⓑ Ⓒ Ⓓ
3. Ⓐ Ⓑ Ⓒ Ⓓ
4. Ⓐ Ⓑ Ⓒ Ⓓ
5. Ⓐ Ⓑ Ⓒ Ⓓ
6. Ⓐ Ⓑ Ⓒ Ⓓ
7. Ⓐ Ⓑ Ⓒ Ⓓ
8. Ⓐ Ⓑ Ⓒ Ⓓ
9. Ⓐ Ⓑ Ⓒ Ⓓ
10. Ⓐ Ⓑ Ⓒ Ⓓ

Test Practice 6

1. Ⓐ Ⓑ Ⓒ Ⓓ
2. Ⓐ Ⓑ Ⓒ Ⓓ
3. Ⓐ Ⓑ Ⓒ Ⓓ
4. Ⓐ Ⓑ Ⓒ Ⓓ
5. Ⓐ Ⓑ Ⓒ Ⓓ
6. Ⓐ Ⓑ Ⓒ Ⓓ
7. Ⓐ Ⓑ Ⓒ Ⓓ
8. Ⓐ Ⓑ Ⓒ Ⓓ
9. Ⓐ Ⓑ Ⓒ Ⓓ
10. Ⓐ Ⓑ Ⓒ Ⓓ

Answer Key

Page 4
1. C
2. B
3. B
4. B
5. a penny
6. a dime

Page 5
1. 5
2. 7
3. 6

Page 6
1. 1¢
2. 25¢
3. 5¢
4. 10¢
5. dime, nickel
6. quarter, penny
7. quarter, penny, dime

Page 7
1. 2¢
2. 10¢
3. 20¢
4. 9¢
5. 8¢
6. 30¢
7. 60¢
8. 50¢
9. penny
10. nickels

Page 8
1. 40¢
2. 27¢
3. 13¢
4. 30¢
5. 25¢
6. 16¢
7. 25¢
8. 55¢
9. 20¢
10. 51¢

Page 9
1. 45¢
2. 75¢
3. 35¢
4. 30¢; yes
5. 36¢; no
6. 30¢

7. 25¢
8. 41¢
9. 5
10. 25

Page 10
1. B
2. B
3. C
4. B

Page 11
1. A
2. D
3. C
4. A
5. D

Page 12
1. A
2. C
3. B
4. A
5. D

Page 13
1. C
2. C
3. A

Page 14
1. 80¢
2. 65¢
3. 60¢
4. 50¢
5. 40¢

Page 15
1. 29¢
2. 29¢
3. 42¢
4. 16¢

Page 16
1. 150¢
2. 104¢
3. 24¢
4. 99¢

Page 17
1. A
2. D
3. A
4. C

Page 18
1. C
2. A
3. D
4. A

Page 19
1. 32¢
2. 20¢
3. 28¢
4. 18¢

Page 20
1. 10¢
2. 9¢
3. 20¢
4. 3¢

Page 21
1. B
2. B
3. A
4. A
5. A

Page 22
1. C
2. C
3. B
4. C

Page 23
1. no
2. no
3. yes
4. no

Page 24
1. E
2. I
3. F
4. B
5. J
6. G
7. C
8. A
9. D
10. H

Page 25
1. B
2. D
3. C
4. $0.42
5. $0.60
6. $0.72

Answer Key

Page 26
1. 42¢
2. 71¢
3. $0.42
4. $0.34

Page 27
1. C
2. D
3. C
4. C
5. D
6. A
7. B

Page 28
1. D
2. C

Page 29
1. B
2. B

Page 30
1. D
2. A
3. D

Page 31
1. $4.20 > $3.45
2. $2.80 > $2.40
3. $4.05 > $2.60
4. $2.70 < $3.75
5. $3.20 < $3.55

Page 32
1. $4.40 > $3.50
2. $3.25 < $3.75
3. $4.55 > $2.55
4. $1.95 < $3.15
5. $3.10 < $3.20

Page 33
1. A
2. B

Page 34
1. B
2. D

Page 35
1. B
2. D

Page 36
1. C
2. C

Page 37
1. yes
2. no
3. 30¢
4. 15¢
5. 42¢
6. 26¢
7. 30¢
8. $1.10

Page 38
1. $1.56
2. $5.25
3. $3.35
4. $4.30
5. $2.80
6. $2.99
7. $5.75
8. $2.35

Page 39
1. $1.85
2. $0.40
3. $0.40
4. $1.40
5. $1.85

Page 40
1. D
2. C
3. D
4. A
5. C
6. C
7. D
8. A
9. D
10. C

Page 41
1. B
2. B
3. A
4. C
5. D
6. D
7. B
8. D
9. B
10. C

Page 42
1. A
2. A
3. C
4. B
5. A
6. C
7. D
8. A
9. B
10. C

Page 43
1. C
2. C
3. B
4. B
5. A
6. B
7. C
8. B
9. A
10. D

Page 44
1. A
2. C
3. B
4. D
5. A
6. A
7. A
8. C
9. B
10. C

Page 45
1. A
2. C
3. D
4. A
5. D
6. A
7. A
8. B
9. A
10. B